The
MESSAGE

PROVERBS

Eugene H. Peterson

NAVPRESS
BRINGING TRUTH TO LIFE
NavPress Publishing Group
P.O. Box 35001, Colorado Springs, Colorado 80935

Old Testament Exegetical Consultant:
   Dr. Robert L. Alden
   Denver Seminary
   Denver, Colorado

Stylistic Consultant:
   Luci Shaw
   president, Shaw Publishers;
   writer-in-residence, Regen College

Library of Congress Catalog Card Number: 95-67772
ISBN 08910-99174

Cover illustration: David Cox, Sr., *View near Bettws-y-
Coed,* 1846, Birmingham Museums and Gallery, Birmingham, England

Printed in the United States of America

1 2 3 4 5 6 7 8 9 10 11 12 13 14 15 / 00 99 98 97 96 95

Published in association with the literary agency of
Alive Communications, P.O. Box 49068, Colorado
Springs, CO 80949.

Proverbs

INTRODUCTION

Many people think that what's written in the Bible has mostly to do with getting people into heaven—getting right with God, saving their eternal souls. It does have to do with that, of course, but not *mostly*. It is equally concerned with living on this earth—living well, living in robust sanity. In our Scriptures, heaven is not the primary concern, to which earth is a tag-along afterthought. "On earth *as* it is in heaven" is Jesus' prayer.

"Wisdom" is the biblical term for this on-earth-as-it-is-in-heaven everyday living. Wisdom is the art of living skillfully in whatever actual conditions we find ourselves. It has virtually nothing to do with information as such, with knowledge as such. A college degree is no certification of wisdom—nor is it primarily concerned with keeping us out of moral mud puddles, although it does have a profound moral effect upon us.

Wisdom has to do with becoming skillful in honoring our parents and raising our children, handling our money and conducting our sexual lives, going to work and exercising leadership, using words well and treating friends kindly, eating and drinking healthily, cultivating emotions within ourselves and attitudes toward others that make for peace. Threaded through all these items is the insistence that the way we think of and respond to God is the most practical thing we do. In matters of everyday practicality, nothing, absolutely nothing, takes precedence over God.

Proverbs concentrates on these concerns more than any other book in the Bible. Attention to the here and now is everywhere present in the stories and legislation, the prayers and the sermons, that are spread over the thousands of pages of the Bible. Proverbs distills it all into riveting images and aphorisms that keep us connected in holy obedience to the ordinary.

WISE SAYINGS OF SOLOMON

1

A MANUAL FOR LIVING

These are the wise sayings of Solomon,
    David's son, Israel's king—
Written down so we'll know how to live well and right,
    to understand what life means and where it's going;
A manual for living,
    for learning what's right and just and fair;
To teach the inexperienced the ropes
    and give our young people a grasp on reality.
There's something here also for seasoned men and women,
    still a thing or two for the experienced to learn—
Fresh wisdom to probe and penetrate,
    the rhymes and reasons of wise men and women.

START WITH GOD

Start with GOD—the first step in learning is bowing down to
        GOD;
    only fools thumb their noses at such wisdom and learning.

Pay close attention, friend, to what your father tells you;
    never forget what you learned at your mother's knee.
Wear their counsel like flowers in your hair,
    like rings on your fingers.
Dear friend, if bad companions tempt you,
    don't go along with them.

If they say—"Let's go out and raise some hell.
  Let's beat up some old man, mug some old woman.
Let's pick them clean
  and get them ready for their funerals.
We'll load up on top-quality loot.
  We'll haul it home by the truckload.
Join us for the time of your life!
  With us, it's share and share alike!"—
Oh, friend, don't give them a second look;
  don't listen to them for a minute.
They're racing to a very bad end,
  hurrying to ruin everything they lay hands on.
Nobody robs a bank
  with everyone watching,
Yet that's what these people are doing—
  they're doing themselves in.
When you grab all you can get, that's what happens:
  the more you get, the less you are.

LADY WISDOM

Lady Wisdom goes out in the street and shouts.
  At the town center she makes her speech.
In the middle of the traffic she takes her stand.
  At the busiest corner she calls out:

"Simpletons! How long will you wallow in ignorance?
  Cynics! How long will you feed your cynicism?
Idiots! How long will you refuse to learn?
  About face! I can revise your life.

Look, I'm ready to pour out my spirit on you;
	I'm ready to tell you all I know.
As it is, I've called, but you've turned a deaf ear;
	I've reached out to you, but you've ignored me.

"Since you laugh at my counsel
	and make a joke of my advice,
How can I take you seriously?
	I'll turn the tables and joke about *your* troubles!
What if the roof falls in,
	and your whole life goes to pieces?
What if catastrophe strikes and there's nothing
	to show for your life but rubble and ashes?
You'll need me then. You'll call for me, but don't expect
		an answer.
	No matter how hard you look, you won't find me.

"Because you hated Knowledge
	and had nothing to do with the Fear-of-GOD,
Because you wouldn't take my advice
	and brushed aside all my offers to train you,
Well, you've made your bed—now lie in it;
	you wanted your own way—now, how do you like it?
Don't you see what happens, you simpletons, you idiots?
	Carelessness kills; complacency is murder.
First pay attention to me, and then relax.
	Now you can take it easy—you're in good hands."

2

MAKE INSIGHT YOUR PRIORITY

Good friend, take to heart what I'm telling you;
    collect my counsels and guard them with your life.
Tune your ears to the world of Wisdom;
    set your heart on a life of Understanding.
That's right—if you make Insight your priority,
    and won't take no for an answer,
Searching for it like a prospector panning for gold,
    like an adventurer on a treasure hunt,
Believe me, before you know it Fear-of-GOD will be yours;
    you'll have come upon the Knowledge of God.

And here's why: GOD gives out Wisdom free,
    is plainspoken in Knowledge and Understanding.
He's a rich mine of Common Sense for those who live well,
    a personal bodyguard to the candid and sincere.
He keeps his eye on all who live honestly,
    and pays special attention to his loyally committed ones.

So now you can pick out what's true and fair,
    find all the good trails!
Lady Wisdom will be your close friend,
    and Brother Knowledge your pleasant companion.
Good Sense will scout ahead for danger,
    Insight will keep an eye out for you.
They'll keep you from making wrong turns,
    or following the bad directions

Of those who are lost themselves
    and can't tell a trail from a tumbleweed,
These losers who make a game of evil
    and throw parties to celebrate perversity,
Traveling paths that go nowhere,
    wandering in a maze of detours and dead ends.

Wise friends will rescue you from the Temptress—
    that smooth-talking Seductress
Who's faithless to the husband she married years ago,
    never gave a second thought to her promises before God.
Her whole way of life is doomed;
    every step she takes brings her closer to hell.
No one who joins her company ever comes back,
    ever sets foot on the path to real living.

So—join the company of good men and women,
    keep your feet on the tried and true paths.
It's the men who walk straight who will settle this land,
    the women with integrity who will last here.
The corrupt will lose their lives;
    the dishonest will be gone for good.

3

DON'T ASSUME YOU KNOW IT ALL

Good friend, don't forget all I've taught you;
    take to heart my commands.
They'll help you live a long, long time,
    a long life lived full and well.

Don't lose your grip on Love and Loyalty.
    Tie them around your neck; carve their initials on your heart.
Earn a reputation for living well
    in God's eyes and the eyes of the people.

Trust GOD from the bottom of your heart;
    don't try to figure out everything on your own.
Listen for GOD's voice in everything you do, everywhere you go;
    he's the one who will keep you on track.
Don't assume that you know it all.
    Run to GOD! Run from evil!
Your body will glow with health,
    your very bones will vibrate with life!
Honor GOD with everything you own;
    give him the first and the best.
Your barns will burst,
    your wine vats will brim over.
But don't, dear friend, resent GOD's discipline;
    don't sulk under his loving correction.
It's the child he loves that GOD corrects;
    a father's delight is behind all this.

THE VERY TREE OF LIFE

You're blessed when you meet Lady Wisdom,
    when you make friends with Madame Insight.
She's worth far more than money in the bank;
    her friendship is better than a big salary.
Her value exceeds all the trappings of wealth;
    nothing you could wish for holds a candle to her.

With one hand she gives long life,
>with the other she confers recognition.
Her manner is beautiful,
>her life wonderfully complete.
She's the very Tree of Life to those who embrace her.
>Hold her tight—and be blessed!

With Lady Wisdom, GOD formed Earth;
>with Madame Insight, he raised Heaven.
They knew when to signal rivers and springs to the surface,
>and dew to descend from the night skies.

NEVER WALK AWAY

Dear friend, guard Clear Thinking and Common Sense with
>your life;
>don't for a minute lose sight of them.
They'll keep your soul alive and well,
>they'll keep you fit and attractive.
You'll travel safely,
>you'll neither tire nor trip.
You'll take afternoon naps without a worry,
>you'll enjoy a good night's sleep.
No need to panic over alarms or surprises,
>or predictions that doomsday's just around the corner,
Because GOD will be right there with you;
>he'll keep you safe and sound.

Never walk away from someone who deserves help;
>your hand is *God's* hand for that person.

Don't tell your neighbor, "Maybe some other time,"
  or, "Try me tomorrow,"
  when the money's right there in your pocket.
Don't figure ways of taking advantage of your neighbor
  when he's sitting there trusting and unsuspecting.

Don't walk around with a chip on your shoulder,
  always spoiling for a fight.
Don't try to be like those who shoulder their way through life.
  Why be a bully?
"Why not?" you say. Because GOD can't stand twisted souls.
  It's the straightforward who get his respect.

GOD's curse blights the house of the wicked,
  but he blesses the home of the righteous.
He gives proud skeptics a cold shoulder,
  but if you're down on your luck, he's right there to help.
Wise living gets rewarded with honor;
  stupid living gets the booby prize.

4

YOUR LIFE IS AT STAKE

Listen, friends, to some fatherly advice;
  sit up and take notice so you'll know how to live.
I'm giving you good counsel;
  don't let it go in one ear and out the other.

When I was a boy at my father's knee,
  the pride and joy of my mother,

He would sit me down and drill me:
    "Take this to heart. Do what I tell you—live!
Sell everything and buy Wisdom! Forage for Understanding!
    Don't forget one word! Don't deviate an inch!
Never walk away from Wisdom—she guards your life;
    love her—she keeps her eye on you.
Above all and before all, do this: Get Wisdom!
    Write this at the top of your list: Get Understanding!
Throw your arms around her—believe me, you won't regret it;
    never let her go—she'll make your life glorious.
She'll garland your life with grace,
    she'll festoon your days with beauty."

Dear friend, take my advice;
    it will add years to your life.
I'm writing out clear directions to Wisdom Way,
    I'm drawing a map to Righteous Road.
I don't want you ending up in blind alleys,
    or wasting time making wrong turns.
Hold tight to good advice; don't relax your grip.
    Guard it well—your life is at stake!
Don't take Wicked Bypass;
    don't so much as set foot on that road.
Stay clear of it; give it a wide berth.
    Make a detour and be on your way.

Evil people are restless
    unless they're making trouble;
They can't get a good night's sleep
    unless they've made life miserable for somebody.

Perversity is their food and drink,
    violence their drug of choice.

The ways of right-living people glow with light;
    the longer they live, the brighter they shine.
But the road of wrongdoing gets darker and darker—
    travelers can't see a thing; they fall flat on their faces.

LEARN IT BY HEART

Dear friend, listen well to my words;
    tune your ears to my voice.
Keep my message in plain view at all times.
    Concentrate! Learn it by heart!
Those who discover these words live, really live;
    body and soul, they're bursting with health.

Keep vigilant watch over your heart;
    that's where life starts.
Don't talk out of both sides of your mouth;
    avoid careless banter, white lies, and gossip.
Keep your eyes straight ahead;
    ignore all sideshow distractions.
Watch your step,
    and the road will stretch out smooth before you.
Look neither right nor left;
    leave evil in the dust.

NOTHING BUT SIN AND BONES

Dear friend, pay close attention to this, my wisdom;
    listen very closely to the way I see it.
Then you'll acquire a taste for good sense;
    what I tell you will keep you out of trouble.

The lips of a seductive woman are oh so sweet,
    her soft words are oh so smooth.
But it won't be long before she's gravel in your mouth,
    a pain in your gut, a wound in your heart.
She's dancing down the primrose path to Death;
    she's headed straight for Hell and taking you with her.
She hasn't a clue about Real Life,
    about who she is or where she's going.

So, my friend, listen closely;
    don't treat my words casually.
Keep your distance from such a woman;
    absolutely stay out of her neighborhood.
You don't want to squander your wonderful life,
    to waste your precious life among the hardhearted.
Why should you allow strangers to take advantage of you?
    Why be exploited by those who care nothing for you?
You don't want to end your life full of regrets,
    nothing but sin and bones,
Saying, "Oh, why didn't I do what they told me?
    Why did I reject a disciplined life?

Why didn't I listen to my mentors,
     or take my teachers seriously?
My life is ruined!
     I haven't one blessed thing to show for my life!"

NEVER TAKE LOVE FOR GRANTED

Do you know the saying, "Drink from your own rain barrel,
     draw water from your own spring-fed well"?
It's true. Otherwise, you may one day come home
     and find your barrel empty and your well polluted.

Your spring water is for you and you only,
     not to be passed around among strangers.
Bless your fresh-flowing fountain!
     Enjoy the wife you married as a young man!
Lovely as an angel, beautiful as a rose—
     don't ever quit taking delight in her body.
     Never take her love for granted!
Why would you trade enduring intimacies for cheap thrills
          with a whore?
     for dalliance with a promiscuous stranger?

Mark well that GOD doesn't miss a move you make;
     he's aware of every step you take.
The shadow of your sin will overtake you;
     you'll find yourself stumbling all over yourself in the dark.
Death is the reward of an undisciplined life;
     your foolish decisions trap you in a dead end.

6

LIKE A DEER FROM THE HUNTER

Dear friend, if you've gone into hock with your neighbor
    or locked yourself into a deal with a stranger,
If you've impulsively promised the shirt off your back
    and now find yourself shivering out in the cold,
Friend, don't waste a minute, get yourself out of that mess.
    You're in that man's clutches!
    Go, put on a long face; act desperate.
Don't procrastinate—
    there's no time to lose.
Run like a deer from the hunter,
    fly like a bird from the trapper!

A LESSON FROM THE ANT

You lazy fool, look at an ant.
    Watch it closely; let it teach you a thing or two.
Nobody has to tell it what to do.
    All summer it stores up food;
    at harvest it stockpiles provisions.
So how long are you going to laze around doing nothing?
    How long before you get out of bed?
A nap here, a nap there, a day off here, a day off there,
    sit back, take it easy—do you know what comes next?
Just this: You can look forward to a dirt-poor life,
    poverty your permanent houseguest!

ALWAYS COOKING UP SOMETHING NASTY

Riffraff and rascals
    talk out of both sides of their mouths.
They wink at each other, they shuffle their feet,
    they cross their fingers behind their backs.
Their perverse minds are always cooking up something nasty,
    always stirring up trouble.
Catastrophe is just around the corner for them,
    a total smash-up, their lives ruined beyond repair.

SEVEN THINGS GOD HATES

Here are six things GOD hates,
    and one more that he loathes with a passion:

        eyes that are arrogant,
        a tongue that lies,
        hands that murder the innocent,
        a heart that hatches evil plots,
        feet that race down a wicked track,
        a mouth that lies under oath,
        a troublemaker in the family.

WARNING ON ADULTERY

Good friend, follow your father's good advice;
    don't wander off from your mother's teachings.
Wrap yourself in them from head to foot;
    wear them like a scarf around your neck.
Wherever you walk, they'll guide you;

whenever you rest, they'll guard you;
   when you wake up, they'll tell you what's next.
For sound advice is a beacon,
   good teaching is a light,
   moral discipline is a life path.

They'll protect you from wanton women,
   from the seductive talk of some temptress.
Don't lustfully fantasize on her beauty,
   nor be taken in by her bedroom eyes.
You can buy an hour with a whore for a loaf of bread,
   but a wanton woman may well eat *you* alive.
Can you build a fire in your lap
   and not burn your pants?
Can you walk barefoot on hot coals
   and not get blisters?
It's the same when you have sex with your neighbor's wife:
   Touch her and you'll pay for it. No excuses.
Hunger is no excuse
   for a thief to steal;
When he's caught he has to pay it back,
   even if he has to put his whole house in hock.
Adultery is a brainless act,
   soul-destroying, self-destructive;
Expect a bloody nose, a black eye,
   and a reputation ruined for good.
For jealousy detonates rage in a cheated husband;
   wild for revenge, he won't make allowances.
Nothing you say or pay will make it all right;
   neither bribes nor reason will satisfy him.

7

DRESSED TO SEDUCE

Dear friend, do what I tell you;
    treasure my careful instructions.
Do what I say and you'll live well.
    My teaching is as precious as your eyesight—guard it!
Write it out on the back of your hands;
    etch it on the chambers of your heart.
Talk to Wisdom as to a sister.
    Treat Insight as your companion.
They'll be with you to fend off the Temptress—
    that smooth-talking, honey-tongued Seductress.

As I stood at the window of my house
    looking out through the shutters,
Watching the mindless crowd stroll by,
    I spotted a young man without any sense
Arriving at the corner of the street where she lived,
    then turning up the path to her house.
It was dusk, the evening coming on,
    the darkness thickening into night.
Just then, a woman met him—
    she'd been lying in wait for him, dressed to seduce him.
Brazen and brash she was,
    restless and roaming, never at home,
Walking the streets, loitering in the mall,
    hanging out at every corner in town.

She threw her arms around him and kissed him,
  boldly took his arm and said,
"I've got all the makings for a feast—
  today I made my offerings, my vows are all paid,
So now I've come to find you,
  hoping to catch sight of your face—and here you are!
I've spread fresh, clean sheets on my bed,
  colorful imported linens.
My bed is aromatic with spices
  and exotic fragrances.
Come, let's make love all night,
  spend the night in ecstatic lovemaking!
My husband's not home; he's away on business,
  and he won't be back for a month."

Soon she has him eating out of her hand,
  bewitched by her honeyed speech.
Before you know it, he's trotting behind her,
  like a calf led to the butcher shop,
Like a stag lured into ambush
  and then shot with an arrow,
Like a bird flying into a net
  not knowing that its flying life is over.

So, friends, listen to me,
  take these words of mine most seriously.
Don't fool around with a woman like that;
  don't even stroll through her neighborhood.
Countless victims come under her spell;
  she's the death of many a poor man.

She runs a halfway house to hell,
    fits you out with a shroud and a coffin.

8

LADY WISDOM CALLS OUT

Do you hear Lady Wisdom calling?
    Can you hear Madame Insight raising her voice?
She's taken her stand at First and Main,
    at the busiest intersection.
Right in the city square
    where the traffic is thickest, she shouts,
"You—I'm talking to all of you,
    everyone out here on the streets!
Listen, you idiots—learn good sense!
    You blockheads—shape up!
Don't miss a word of this—I'm telling you how to live well,
    I'm telling you how to live at your best.
My mouth chews and savors and relishes truth—
    I can't stand the taste of evil!
You'll only hear true and right words from my mouth;
    not one syllable will be twisted or skewed.
You'll recognize this as true—you with open minds;
    truth-ready minds will see it at once.
Prefer my life-disciplines over chasing after money,
    and God-knowledge over a lucrative career.
For Wisdom is better than all the trappings of wealth;
    nothing you could wish for holds a candle to her.

"I am Lady Wisdom, and I live next to Sanity;
    Knowledge and Discretion live just down the street.
The Fear-of-GOD means hating Evil,
    whose ways I hate with a passion—
    pride and arrogance and crooked talk.
Good counsel and common sense are my characteristics;
    I am both Insight and the Virtue to live it out.
With my help, leaders rule,
    and lawmakers legislate fairly;
With my help, governors govern,
    along with all in legitimate authority.
I love those who love me;
    those who look for me find me.
Wealth and Glory accompany me—
    also substantial Honor and a Good Name.
My benefits are worth more than a big salary, even a *very* big
        salary;
    the returns on me exceed any imaginable bonus.
You can find me on Righteous Road—that's where I walk—
    at the intersection of Justice Avenue,
Handing out life to those who love me,
    filling their arms with life—armloads of life!

"GOD sovereignly made me—the first, the basic—
    before he did anything else.
I was brought into being a long time ago,
    well before Earth got its start.
I arrived on the scene before Ocean,
    yes, even before Springs and Rivers and Lakes.

Before Mountains were sculpted and Hills took shape,
    I was already there, newborn;
Long before GOD stretched out Earth's Horizons,
    and tended to the minute details of Soil and Weather,
And set Sky firmly in place,
    I was there.
When he mapped and gave borders to wild Ocean,
    built the vast vault of Heaven,
    and installed the fountains that fed Ocean,
When he drew a boundary for Sea,
    posted a sign that said, NO TRESPASSING,
And then staked out Earth's foundations,
    I was right there with him, making sure everything fit.
Day after day I was there, with my joyful applause,
    always enjoying his company,
Delighted with the world of things and creatures,
    happily celebrating the human family.

"So, my dear friends, listen carefully;
    those who embrace these my ways are most blessed.
Mark a life of discipline and live wisely;
    don't squander your precious life.
Blessed the man, blessed the woman, who listens to me,
    awake and ready for me each morning,
    alert and responsive as I start my day's work.
When you find me, you find life, real life,
    to say nothing of GOD's good pleasure.
But if you wrong me, you damage your very soul;
    when you reject me, you're flirting with death."

9
Lady Wisdom Gives a Dinner Party

Lady Wisdom has built and furnished her home;
    it's supported by seven hewn timbers.
The banquet meal is ready to be served: lamb roasted,
    wine poured out, table set with silver and flowers.
Having dismissed her serving maids,
    Lady Wisdom goes to town, stands in a prominent place,
    and invites everyone within sound of her voice:
"Are you confused about life, don't know what's going on?
    Come with me, oh come, have dinner with me!
I've prepared a wonderful spread—fresh-baked bread,
    roast lamb, carefully selected wines.
Leave your impoverished confusion and *live!*
    Walk up the street to a life with meaning."

☩

If you reason with an arrogant cynic, you'll get slapped in the
    face;
    confront bad behavior and get a kick in the shins.
So don't waste your time on a scoffer;
    all you'll get for your pains is abuse.
But if you correct those who care about life,
    that's different—they'll love you for it!
Save your breath for the wise—they'll be wiser for it;
    tell good people what you know—they'll profit from it.
Skilled living gets its start in the Fear-of-God,
    insight into life from knowing a Holy God.

It's through me, Lady Wisdom, that your life deepens,
    and the years of your life ripen.
Live wisely and wisdom will permeate your life;
    mock life and life will mock you.

MADAME WHORE CALLS OUT, TOO

Then there's this other woman, Madame Whore—
    brazen, empty-headed, frivolous.
She sits on the front porch
    of her house on Main Street,
And as people walk by minding
    their own business, calls out,
"Are you confused about life, don't know what's going on?
    Steal off with me, I'll show you a good time!
    No one will ever know—I'll give you the time of your life."
But they don't know about all the skeletons in her closet,
    that all her guests end up in hell.

THE WISE SAYINGS OF SOLOMON

10

AN HONEST LIFE IS IMMORTAL

Wise son, glad father;
    stupid son, sad mother.

Ill-gotten gain gets you nowhere;
    an honest life is immortal.

GOD won't starve an honest soul,
    but he frustrates the appetites of the wicked.

Sloth makes you poor;
    diligence brings wealth.

Make hay while the sun shines—that's smart;
    go fishing during harvest—that's stupid.

Blessings accrue on a good and honest life,
    but the mouth of the wicked is a dark cave of abuse.

A good and honest life is a blessed memorial;
    a wicked life leaves a rotten stench.

A wise heart takes orders;
    an empty head will come unglued.

Honesty lives confident and carefree,
    but Shifty is sure to be exposed.

An evasive eye is a sign of trouble ahead,
    but an open, face-to-face meeting results in peace.

The mouth of a good person is a deep, life-giving well,
    but the mouth of the wicked is a dark cave of abuse.

Hatred starts fights,
    but love pulls a quilt over the bickering.

Proverbs 10:13

You'll find wisdom on the lips of a person of insight,
  but the shortsighted needs a slap in the face.

The wise accumulate knowledge—a true treasure;
  know-it-alls talk too much—a sheer waste.

THE ROAD TO LIFE IS A DISCIPLINED LIFE

The wealth of the rich is their bastion;
  the poverty of the indigent is their ruin.

The wage of a good person is exuberant life;
  an evil person ends up with nothing but sin.

The road to life is a disciplined life;
  ignore correction and you're lost for good.

Liars secretly hoard hatred;
  fools openly spread slander.

The more talk, the less truth;
  the wise measure their words.

The speech of a good person is worth waiting for;
  the blabber of the wicked is worthless.

The talk of a good person is rich fare for many,
  but chatterboxes die of an empty heart.

FEAR-OF-GOD EXPANDS YOUR LIFE

GOD's blessing makes life rich;
    nothing we do can improve on GOD.

An empty-head thinks mischief is fun,
    but a mindful person relishes wisdom.

The nightmares of the wicked come true;
    what the good people desire, they get.

When the storm is over, there's nothing left of the wicked;
    good people, firm on their rock foundation, aren't even
        fazed.

A lazy employee will give you nothing but trouble;
    it's vinegar in the mouth, smoke in the eyes.

The Fear-of-GOD expands your life;
    a wicked life is a puny life.

The aspirations of good people end in celebration;
    the ambitions of bad people crash.

GOD is solid backing to a well-lived life,
    but he calls into question a shabby performance.

Good people *last*—they can't be moved;
    the wicked are here today, gone tomorrow.

A good person's mouth is a clear fountain of wisdom;
    a foul mouth is a stagnant swamp.

The speech of a good person clears the air;
    the words of the wicked pollute it.

11

WITHOUT GOOD DIRECTION, PEOPLE LOSE THEIR WAY

GOD hates cheating in the marketplace;
    he loves it when business is aboveboard.

The stuck-up fall flat on their faces,
    but down-to-earth people stand firm.

The integrity of the honest keeps them on track;
    the deviousness of crooks brings them to ruin.

A thick bankroll is no help when life falls apart,
    but a principled life can stand up to the worst.

Moral character makes for smooth traveling;
    an evil life is a hard life.

Good character is the best insurance;
    crooks get trapped in their sinful lust.

When the wicked die, that's it—
    the story's over, end of hope.

A good person is saved from much trouble;
    a bad person runs straight into it.

The loose tongue of the godless spreads destruction;
    the common sense of the godly preserves them.

When it goes well for good people, the whole town cheers;
    when it goes badly for bad people, the town celebrates.

When right-living people bless the city, it flourishes;
    evil talk turns it into a ghost town in no time.

Mean-spirited slander is heartless;
    quiet discretion accompanies good sense.

A gadabout gossip can't be trusted with a secret,
    but someone of integrity won't violate a confidence.

Without good direction, people lose their way;
    the more wise counsel you follow, the better your chances.

Whoever makes deals with strangers is sure to get burned;
    if you keep a cool head, you'll avoid rash bargains.

A woman of gentle grace gets respect,
    but men of rough violence grab for loot.

A GOD-SHAPED LIFE

When you're kind to others, you help yourself;
    when you're cruel to others, you hurt yourself.

Bad work gets paid with a bad check;
    good work gets solid pay.

Take your stand with God's loyal community and live,
    or chase after phantoms of evil and die.

GOD can't stand deceivers,
    but oh how he relishes integrity.

Count on this: The wicked won't get off scot-free,
    and God's loyal people will triumph.

Like a gold ring in a pig's snout
    is a beautiful face on an empty head.

The desires of good people lead straight to the best,
    but wicked ambition ends in angry frustration.

The world of the generous gets larger and larger;
    the world of the stingy gets smaller and smaller.

The one who blesses others is abundantly blessed;
    those who help others are helped.

Curses on those who drive a hard bargain!
    Blessings on all who play fair and square!

The one who seeks good finds delight;
    the student of evil becomes evil.

A life devoted to things is a dead life, a stump;
    a God-shaped life is a flourishing tree.

Exploit or abuse your family, and end up with a fistful of air;
    common sense tells you it's a stupid way to live.

A good life is a fruit-bearing tree;
    a violent life destroys souls.

If good people barely make it,
    what's in store for the bad!

12

IF YOU LOVE LEARNING

If you love learning, you love the discipline that goes with it—
    how shortsighted to refuse correction!

A good person basks in the delight of GOD,
    and he wants nothing to do with devious schemers.

3 You can't find firm footing in a swamp,
    but life rooted in God stands firm.

A hearty wife invigorates her husband,
    but a frigid woman is cancer in the bones.

The thinking of principled people makes for justice;
    the plots of degenerates corrupt.

6   The words of the wicked kill;
      the speech of the upright saves.

Wicked people fall to pieces—there's nothing to them;
      the homes of good people hold together.

A person who talks sense is honored;
      airheads are held in contempt.

Better to be ordinary and work for a living
      than act important and starve in the process.

10   Good people are good to their animals;
      the "good-hearted" bad people kick and abuse them.

The one who stays on the job has food on the table;
      the witless chase whims and fancies.

What the wicked construct finally falls into ruin,
      while the roots of the righteous give life, and more life.

WISE PEOPLE TAKE ADVICE

The gossip of bad people gets them in trouble;
      the conversation of good people keeps them out of it.

14   Well-spoken words bring satisfaction;
      well-done work has its own reward.

Fools are headstrong and do what they like;
      wise people take advice.

Fools have short fuses and explode all too quickly;
    the prudent quietly shrug off insults.

Truthful witness by a good person clears the air,
    but liars lay down a smoke screen of deceit.

Rash language cuts and maims,
    but there is healing in the words of the wise.

19 Truth lasts;
    lies are here today, gone tomorrow.

Evil scheming distorts the schemer;
    peace-planning brings joy to the planner.

No evil can overwhelm a good person,
    but the wicked have their hands full of it.

God can't stomach liars;
    he loves the company of those who keep their word.

23 Prudent people don't flaunt their knowledge;
    talkative fools broadcast their silliness.

The diligent find freedom in their work;
    the lazy are oppressed by work.

Worry weighs us down;
    a cheerful word picks us up.

Proverbs 12:26

A good person survives misfortune,
    but a wicked life invites disaster.

27 A lazy life is an empty life,
    but "early to rise" gets the job done.

Good men and women travel right into life;
    sin's detours take you straight to hell.

13

WALK WITH THE WISE

Intelligent children listen to their parents;
    foolish children do their own thing.

The good acquire a taste for helpful conversation;
    bullies push and shove their way through life.

Careful words make for a careful life;
    careless talk may ruin everything.

4 Indolence wants it all and gets nothing;
    the energetic have something to show for their lives.

A good person hates false talk;
    a bad person wallows in gibberish.

A God-loyal life keeps you on track;
    sin dumps the wicked in the ditch.

A pretentious, showy life is an empty life;
    a plain and simple life is a full life.

8 The rich can be sued for everything they have,
    but the poor are free of such threats.

The lives of good people are brightly lit streets;
    the lives of the wicked are dark alleys.

Arrogant know-it-alls stir up discord,
    but wise men and women listen to each other's counsel.

Easy come, easy go,
    but steady diligence pays off.

12 Unrelenting disappointment leaves you heartsick,
    but a sudden good break can turn life around.

Ignore the Word and suffer;
    honor God's commands and grow rich.

The teaching of the wise is a fountain of life,
    so, no more drinking from death-tainted wells!

Sound thinking makes for gracious living,
    but liars walk a rough road.

16 A commonsense person *lives* good sense;
    fools litter the country with silliness.

Proverbs 13:17

Irresponsible talk makes a real mess of things,
    but a reliable reporter is a healing presence.

18 Refuse discipline and end up homeless;
    embrace correction and live an honored life.

Souls who follow their hearts thrive;
    fools bent on evil despise matters of soul.

Become wise by walking with the wise;
    hang out with fools and watch your life fall to pieces.

Disaster entraps sinners,
    but God-loyal people get a good life.

22 A good life gets passed on to the grandchildren;
    ill-gotten wealth ends up with good people.

Banks foreclose on the farms of the poor,
    or else the poor lose their shirts to crooked lawyers.

A refusal to correct is a refusal to love;
    love your children by disciplining them.

An appetite for good brings much satisfaction,
    but the belly of the wicked always wants more.

14

A WAY THAT LEADS TO HELL

Lady Wisdom builds a lovely home;
  Sir Fool comes along and tears it down brick by brick.

An honest life shows respect for GOD;
  a degenerate life is a slap in his face.

Frivolous talk provokes a derisive smile;
  wise speech evokes nothing but respect.

No cattle, no crops;
  a good harvest requires a strong ox for the plow.

A true witness never lies;
  a false witness makes a business of it.

Cynics look high and low for wisdom—and never find it;
  the open-minded find it right on their doorstep!

Escape quickly from the company of fools;
  they're a waste of your time, a waste of your words.

The wisdom of the wise keeps life on track;
  the foolishness of fools lands them in the ditch.

The stupid ridicule right and wrong,
  but a moral life is a favored life.

10 The person who shuns the bitter moments of friends
    will be an outsider at their celebrations.

Lives of careless wrongdoing are tumbledown shacks;
    holy living builds soaring cathedrals.

12 There's a way of life that looks harmless enough;
    look again—it leads straight to hell.
13 Sure, those people appear to be having a good time,
    but all that laughter will end in heartbreak.

SIFT AND WEIGH EVERY WORD

A mean person gets paid back in meanness,
    a gracious person in grace.

The gullible believe anything they're told;
    the prudent sift and weigh every word.

The wise watch their steps and avoid evil;
    fools are headstrong and reckless.

17 The hotheaded do things they'll later regret;
    the coldhearted get the cold shoulder.

Foolish dreamers live in a world of illusion;
    wise realists plant their feet on the ground.

Eventually, evil will pay tribute to good;
    the wicked will respect God-loyal people.

An unlucky loser is shunned by all,
    but everyone loves a winner.

21 It's criminal to ignore a neighbor in need,
    but compassion for the poor—what a blessing!

Isn't it obvious that conspirators lose out,
    while the thoughtful win love and trust?

Hard work always pays off;
    mere talk puts no bread on the table.

24 The wise accumulate wisdom;
    fools get stupider by the day.

Souls are saved by truthful witness
    and betrayed by the spread of lies.

26 The Fear-of-God builds up confidence,
    and makes a world safe for your children.

The Fear-of-God is a spring of living water
    so you won't go off drinking from poisoned wells.

The mark of a good leader is loyal followers;
    leadership is nothing without a following.

29 Slowness to anger makes for deep understanding;
    a quick-tempered person stockpiles stupidity.

Proverbs 14:30

A sound mind makes for a robust body,
    but runaway emotions corrode the bones.

You insult your Maker when you exploit the powerless;
    when you're kind to the poor, you honor God.

The evil of bad people leaves them out in the cold;
    the integrity of good people creates a safe place for
        living.

Lady Wisdom is at home in an understanding heart—
    fools never even get to say hello.

God-devotion makes a country strong;
    God-avoidance leaves people weak.

Diligent work gets a warm commendation;
    shiftless work earns an angry rebuke.

15

GOD DOESN'T MISS A THING

A gentle response defuses anger,
    but a sharp tongue kindles a temper-fire.

Knowledge flows like spring water from the wise;
    fools are leaky faucets, dripping nonsense.

GOD doesn't miss a thing—
    he's alert to good and evil alike.

Kind words heal and help;
    cutting words wound and maim.

Moral dropouts won't listen to their elders;
    welcoming correction is a mark of good sense.

The lives of God-loyal people flourish;
    a misspent life is soon bankrupt.

Perceptive words spread knowledge;
    fools are hollow—there's nothing to them.

GOD can't stand pious poses,
    but he delights in genuine prayers.

A life frittered away disgusts GOD;
    he loves those who run straight for the finish line.

It's a school of hard knocks for those who leave God's path,
    a dead-end street for those who hate God's rules.

Even hell holds no secrets from GOD—
    do you think he can't read human hearts?

LIFE ASCENDS TO THE HEIGHTS

Know-it-alls don't like being told what to do;
    they avoid the company of wise men and women.

A cheerful heart brings a smile to your face;
    a sad heart makes it hard to get through the day.

An intelligent person is always eager to take in more truth;
    fools feed on fast-food fads and fancies.

A miserable heart means a miserable life;
    a cheerful heart fills the day with song.

A simple life in the Fear-of-GOD
    is better than a rich life with a ton of headaches.

Better a bread crust shared in love
    than a slab of prime rib served in hate.

Hot tempers start fights;
    a calm, cool spirit keeps the peace.

The path of lazy people is overgrown with briers;
    the diligent walk down a smooth road.

Intelligent children make their parents proud;
    lazy students embarrass their parents.

The empty-headed treat life as a plaything;
    the perceptive grasp its meaning and make a go of it.

Refuse good advice and watch your plans fail;
    take good counsel and watch them succeed.

Congenial conversation—what a pleasure!
    The right word at the right time—beautiful!

Life ascends to the heights for the thoughtful—
    it's a clean about-face from descent into hell.

GOD smashes the pretensions of the arrogant;
    he stands with those who have no standing.

GOD can't stand evil scheming,
    but he puts words of grace and beauty on display.

A greedy and grasping person destroys community;
    those who refuse to exploit live and let live.

Prayerful answers come from God-loyal people;
    the wicked are sewers of abuse.

GOD keeps his distance from the wicked;
    he closely attends to the prayers of God-loyal people.

A twinkle in the eye means joy in the heart,
    and good news makes you feel fit as a fiddle.

Listen to good advice if you want to live well,
    an honored guest among wise men and women.

An undisciplined, self-willed life is puny;
    an obedient, God-willed life is spacious.

Fear-of-GOD is a school in skilled living—
>   first you learn humility, then you experience glory.

16

EVERYTHING WITH A PLACE AND A PURPOSE

Mortals make elaborate plans,
>   but GOD has the last word.

Humans are satisfied with whatever looks good;
>   GOD probes for what *is* good.

Put GOD in charge of your work,
>   then what you've planned will take place.

GOD made everything with a place and purpose;
>   even the wicked are included—but for *judgment*.

GOD can't stomach arrogance or pretense;
>   believe me, he'll put those upstarts in their place.

Guilt is banished through love and truth;
>   Fear-of-GOD deflects evil.

When GOD approves of your life,
>   even your enemies will end up shaking your hand.

Far better to be right and poor
>   than to be wrong and rich.

We plan the way we want to live,
> but only GOD makes us able to live it.

IT PAYS TO TAKE LIFE SERIOUSLY

A good leader motivates,
> doesn't mislead, doesn't exploit.

GOD cares about honesty in the workplace;
> your business is his business.

Good leaders abhor wrongdoing of all kinds;
> sound leadership has a moral foundation.

Good leaders cultivate honest speech;
> they love advisors who tell them the truth.

An intemperate leader wreaks havoc in lives;
> you're smart to stay clear of someone like that.

Good-tempered leaders invigorate lives;
> they're like spring rain and sunshine.

Get wisdom—it's worth more than money;
> choose insight over income every time.

The road of right living bypasses evil;
> watch your step and save your life.

First pride, then the crash—
> the bigger the ego, the harder the fall.

Proverbs 16:19

It's better to live humbly among the poor
    than to live it up among the rich and famous.

It pays to take life seriously;
    things work out when you trust in GOD.

A wise person gets known for insight;
    gracious words add to one's reputation.

True intelligence is a spring of fresh water,
    while fools sweat it out the hard way.

They make a lot of sense, these wise folks;
    whenever they speak, their reputation increases.

Gracious speech is like clover honey—
    good taste to the soul, quick energy for the body.

There's a way that looks harmless enough;
    look again—it leads straight to hell.

Appetite is an incentive to work;
    hunger makes you work all the harder.

Mean people spread mean gossip;
    their words smart and burn.

Troublemakers start fights;
    gossips break up friendships.

Calloused climbers betray their very own friends;
    they'd stab their own grandmothers in the back.

A shifty eye betrays an evil intention;
    a clenched jaw signals trouble ahead.

Gray hair is a mark of distinction,
    the award for a God-loyal life.

Moderation is better than muscle,
    self-control better than political power.

Make your motions and cast your votes,
    but GOD has the final say.

17

A WHACK ON THE HEAD OF A FOOL

A meal of bread and water in contented peace
    is better than a banquet spiced with quarrels.

A wise servant takes charge of an unruly child
    and is honored as one of the family.

As silver in a crucible and gold in a pan,
    so our lives are assayed by GOD.

Evil people relish malicious conversation;
    the ears of liars itch for dirty gossip.

Whoever mocks poor people, insults their Creator;
    gloating over misfortune is a punishable crime.

Old people are distinguished by grandchildren;
    children take pride in their parents.

We don't expect eloquence from fools,
    nor do we expect lies from our leaders.

Receiving a gift is like getting a rare gemstone;
    any way you look at it, you see beauty refracted.

Overlook an offense and bond a friendship;
    fasten on to a slight and—goodbye, friend!

A quiet rebuke to a person of good sense
    does more than a whack on the head of a fool.

Criminals out looking for nothing but trouble
    won't have to wait long—they'll meet it coming and going!

Better to meet a grizzly robbed of her cubs
    than a fool hellbent on folly.

Those who return evil for good
    will meet their own evil returning.

The start of a quarrel is like a leak in a dam,
    so stop it before it bursts.

Whitewashing bad people and throwing mud on good people
    are equally abhorrent to GOD.

What's this? Fools out shopping for wisdom!
    They wouldn't recognize it if they saw it!

ONE WHO KNOWS MUCH SAYS LITTLE

Friends love through all kinds of weather,
    and families stick together in all kinds of trouble.

It's stupid to try to get something for nothing,
    or run up huge bills you can never pay.

The person who courts sin, marries trouble;
    build a wall, invite a burglar.

A bad motive can't achieve a good end;
    double-talk brings you double trouble.

Having a fool for a child is misery;
    it's no fun being the parent of a dolt.

A cheerful disposition is good for your health;
    gloom and doom leave you bone-tired.

The wicked take bribes under the table;
    they show nothing but contempt for justice.

The perceptive find wisdom in their own front yard;
    fools look for it everywhere but right here.

A surly, stupid child is sheer pain to a father,
    a bitter pill for a mother to swallow.

It's wrong to penalize good behavior,
    or make good citizens pay for the crimes of others.

The one who knows much says little;
    an understanding person remains calm.

Even dunces who keep quiet are thought to be wise;
    as long as they keep their mouths shut, they're smart.

18

Words Kill, Words Give Life

Loners who care only for themselves
    spit on the common good.

Fools care nothing for thoughtful discourse;
    all they do is run off at the mouth.

When wickedness arrives, shame's not far behind;
    contempt for life is contemptible.

Many words rush along like rivers in flood,
    but deep wisdom flows up from artesian springs.

It's not right to go easy on the guilty,
    or come down hard on the innocent.

The words of a fool start fights;
    do him a favor and gag him.

Fools are undone by their big mouths;
    their souls are crushed by their words.

Listening to gossip is like eating cheap candy;
    do you really want junk like that in your belly?

Slack habits and sloppy work
    are as bad as vandalism.

GOD's name is a place of protection—
    good people can run there and be safe.

The rich think their wealth protects them;
    they imagine themselves safe behind it.

Pride first, then the crash,
    but humility is precursor to honor.

Answering before listening
    is both stupid and rude.

A healthy spirit conquers adversity,
    but what can you do when the spirit is crushed?

Proverbs 18:15

Wise men and women are always learning,
 always listening for fresh insights.

A gift gets attention;
 it buys the attention of eminent people.

The first speech in a court case is always convincing—
 until the cross-examination starts!

You may have to draw straws
 when faced with a tough decision.

Do a favor and win a friend forever;
 nothing can untie that bond.

Words satisfy the mind as much as fruit does the stomach;
 good talk is as gratifying as a good harvest.

Words kill, words give life;
 they're either poison or fruit—you choose.

Find a good spouse, you find a good life—
 and even more: the favor of GOD!

The poor speak in soft supplications;
 the rich bark out answers.

Friends come and friends go,
 but a true friend sticks by you like family.

19

IF YOU QUIT LISTENING

Better to be poor and honest
    than a rich person no one can trust.

Ignorant zeal is worthless;
    haste makes waste.

People ruin their lives by their own stupidity,
    so why does GOD always get blamed?

Wealth attracts friends as honey draws flies,
    but poor people are avoided like a plague.

Perjury won't go unpunished.
    Would you let a liar go free?

Lots of people flock around a generous person;
    everyone's a friend to the philanthropist.

When you're down on your luck, even your family avoids you—
    yes, even your best friends wish you'd get lost.
If they see you coming, they look the other way—
    out of sight, out of mind.

Grow a wise heart—you'll do yourself a favor;
    keep a clear head—you'll find a good life.

The person who tells lies gets caught;
    the person who spreads rumors is ruined.

Blockheads shouldn't live on easy street
    any more than workers should give orders to their boss.

Smart people know how to hold their tongue;
    their grandeur is to forgive and forget.

Mean-tempered leaders are like mad dogs;
    the good-natured are like fresh morning dew.

A parent is worn to a frazzle by a stupid child;
    a nagging spouse is a leaky faucet.

House and land are handed down from parents,
    but a congenial spouse comes straight from GOD.

Life collapses on loafers;
    lazybones go hungry.

Keep the rules and keep your life;
    careless living kills.

Mercy to the needy is a loan to GOD,
    and GOD pays back those loans in full.

Discipline your children while you still have the chance;
    indulging them destroys them.

Let angry people endure the backlash of their own anger;
    if you try to make it better, you'll only make it worse.

Take good counsel and accept correction—
    that's the way to live wisely and well.

We humans keep brainstorming options and plans,
    but GOD's purpose prevails.

It's only human to want to make a buck,
    but it's better to be poor than a liar.

Fear-of-GOD is life itself,
    a full life, and serene—no nasty surprises.

Some people dig a fork into the pie
    but are too lazy to raise it to their mouth.

Punish the insolent—make an example of them.
    Who knows? Somebody might learn a good lesson.

Kids who lash out against their parents
    are an embarrassment and disgrace.

If you quit listening, dear child, and strike off on your own,
    you'll soon be out of your depth.

An unprincipled witness desecrates justice;
    the mouths of the wicked spew malice.

The irreverent have to learn reverence the hard way;
only a slap in the face brings fools to attention.

20

DEEP WATER IN THE HEART

Wine makes you mean, beer makes you quarrelsome—
a staggering drunk is not much fun.

Quick-tempered leaders are like mad dogs—
cross them and they bite your head off.

It's a mark of good character to avert quarrels,
but fools love to pick fights.

A farmer too lazy to plant in the spring
has nothing to harvest in the fall.

Knowing what is right is like deep water in the heart;
a wise person draws from the well within.

Lots of people claim to be loyal and loving,
but where on earth can you find one?

God-loyal people, living honest lives,
make it much easier for their children.

Leaders who know their business and care
keep a sharp eye out for the shoddy and cheap,

For who among us can be trusted
   to be always diligent and honest?

Switching price tags and padding the expense account
   are two things GOD hates.

Young people eventually reveal by their actions
   if their motives are on the up and up.

DRINKING FROM THE CHALICE OF KNOWLEDGE

Ears that hear and eyes that see—
   we get our basic equipment from GOD!

Don't be too fond of sleep; you'll end up in the poorhouse.
   Wake up and get up; then there'll be food on the table.

The shopper says, "That's junk—I'll take it off your hands,"
   then goes off boasting of the bargain.

Drinking from the beautiful chalice of knowledge
   is better than adorning oneself with gold and rare gems.

Hold tight to collateral on any loan to a stranger;
   beware of accepting what a transient has pawned.

Stolen bread tastes sweet,
   but soon your mouth is full of gravel.

Form your purpose by asking for counsel,
    then carry it out using all the help you can get.

Gossips can't keep secrets,
    so never confide in blabbermouths.

Anyone who curses father and mother
    extinguishes light and exists benighted.

THE VERY STEPS WE TAKE

A bonanza at the beginning
    is no guarantee of blessing at the end.

Don't ever say, "I'll get you for that!"
    Wait for GOD; he'll settle the score.

GOD hates cheating in the marketplace;
    rigged scales are an outrage.

The very steps we take come from GOD;
    otherwise how would we know where we're going?

An impulsive vow is a trap;
    later you'll wish you could get out of it.

After careful scrutiny, a wise leader
    makes a clean sweep of rebels and dolts.

GOD is in charge of human life,
    watching and examining us inside and out.

Love and truth form a good leader;
 sound leadership is founded on loving integrity.

Youth may be admired for vigor,
 but gray hair gives prestige to old age.

A good thrashing purges evil;
 punishment goes deep within us.

21

GOD EXAMINES OUR MOTIVES

Good leadership is a channel of water controlled by GOD;
 he directs it to whatever ends he chooses.

We justify our actions by appearances;
 GOD examines our motives.

Clean living before God and justice with our neighbors
 mean far more to GOD than religious performance.

Arrogance and pride—distinguishing marks in the wicked—
 are just plain sin.

Careful planning puts you ahead in the long run;
 hurry and scurry puts you further behind.

Make it to the top by lying and cheating;
 get paid with smoke and a promotion—to death!

Proverbs 21:7

The wicked get buried alive by their loot
 because they refuse to use it to help others.

Mixed motives twist life into tangles;
 pure motives take you straight down the road.

DO YOUR BEST, PREPARE FOR THE WORST

Better to live alone in a tumbledown shack
 than share a mansion with a nagging spouse.

Wicked souls love to make trouble;
 they feel nothing for friends and neighbors.

Simpletons only learn the hard way,
 but the wise learn by listening.

A God-loyal person will see right through the wicked
 and undo the evil they've planned.

If you stop your ears to the cries of the poor,
 your cries will go unheard, unanswered.

A quietly given gift soothes an irritable person;
 a heartfelt present cools a hot temper.

Good people celebrate when justice triumphs,
 but for the workers of evil it's a bad day.

Whoever wanders off the straight and narrow
  ends up in a congregation of ghosts.

You're addicted to thrills? What an empty life!
  The pursuit of pleasure is never satisfied.

What a bad person plots against the good, boomerangs;
  the plotter gets it in the end.

Better to live in a tent in the wild
  than with a cross and petulant spouse.

Valuables are safe in a wise person's home;
  fools put it all out for yard sales.

Whoever goes hunting for what is right and kind
  finds life itself—*glorious* life!

One sage entered a whole city of armed soldiers—
  their trusted defenses fell to pieces!

Watch your words and hold your tongue;
  you'll save yourself a lot of grief.

You know their names—Brash, Impudent, Blasphemer—
  intemperate hotheads, every one.

Lazy people finally die of hunger
  because they won't get up and go to work.

Sinners are always wanting what they don't have;
  the God-loyal are always giving what they do have.

27 Religious performance by the wicked stinks;
    it's even worse when they use it to get ahead.

A lying witness is unconvincing;
    a person who speaks truth is respected.

Unscrupulous people fake it a lot;
    honest people are sure of their steps.

Nothing clever, nothing conceived, nothing contrived,
    can get the better of GOD.

Do your best, prepare for the worst—
    then trust GOD to bring victory.

22

THE CURE COMES THROUGH DISCIPLINE

A sterling reputation is better than striking it rich;
    a gracious spirit is better than money in the bank.

The rich and the poor shake hands as equals—
    GOD made them both!

A prudent person sees trouble coming and ducks;
    a simpleton walks in blindly and is clobbered.

4 The payoff for meekness and Fear-of-GOD
    is plenty and honor and a satisfying life.

The perverse travel a dangerous road, potholed and mud-slick;
    if you know what's good for you, stay clear of it.

Point your kids in the right direction—
    when they're old they won't be lost.

The poor are always ruled over by the rich,
    so don't borrow and put yourself under their power.

Whoever sows sin reaps weeds,
    and bullying anger sputters into nothing.

Generous hands are blessed hands
    because they give bread to the poor.

Kick out the troublemakers and things will quiet down;
    you need a break from bickering and griping!

GOD loves the pure-hearted and well-spoken;
    good leaders also delight in their friendship.

GOD guards knowledge with a passion,
    but he'll have nothing to do with deception.

The loafer says, "There's a lion on the loose!
    If I go out I'll be eaten alive!"

The mouth of a whore is a bottomless pit;
    you'll fall in that pit if you're on the outs with GOD.

15 Young people are prone to foolishness and fads;
      the cure comes through tough-minded discipline.

Exploit the poor or glad-hand the rich—whichever,
      you'll end up the poorer for it.

THE THIRTY PRECEPTS OF THE SAGES

DON'T MOVE BACK THE BOUNDARY LINES
Listen carefully to my wisdom;
      take to heart what I can teach you.
You'll treasure its sweetness deep within;
      you'll give it bold expression in your speech.
I'm giving you thirty sterling principles—
      tested guidelines to live by.
Believe me—these are truths that work,
      and will keep you accountable
      to those who sent you.

1

Don't walk on the poor just because they're poor,
      and don't use your position to crush the weak,
Because GOD will come to their defense;
      the life you took, he'll take from you and give back
        to them.

2

Don't hang out with angry people;
      don't keep company with hotheads.

Bad temper is contagious—
    don't get infected.

3

Don't gamble on the pot of gold at the end of the rainbow,
    hocking your house against a lucky chance.
The time will come when you have to pay up;
    you'll be left with nothing but the shirt on your back.

4

Don't stealthily move back the boundary lines
    staked out long ago by your ancestors.

5

Observe people who are good at their work—
    skilled workers are always in demand and admired;
    they don't take a back seat to anyone.

23

RESTRAIN YOURSELF

6

When you go out to dinner with an influential person,
    mind your manners:
Don't gobble your food,
    don't talk with your mouth full.
And don't stuff yourself;
    bridle your appetite.

7

Don't wear yourself out trying to get rich;
    restrain yourself!
Riches disappear in the blink of an eye;
    wealth sprouts wings
    and flies off into the wild blue yonder.

8

Don't accept a meal from a tightwad;
    don't expect anything special.
He'll be as stingy with you as he is with himself;
    he'll say, "Eat! Drink!" but won't mean a word of it.
His miserly serving will turn your stomach
    when you realize the meal's a sham.

9

Don't bother talking sense to fools;
    they'll only poke fun at your words.

10

Don't stealthily move back the boundary lines
    or cheat orphans out of their property,
For they have a powerful Advocate
    who will go to bat for them.

11

Give yourselves to disciplined instruction;
    open your ears to tested knowledge.

12

Don't be afraid to correct your young ones;   *13*
    a spanking won't kill them.
A good spanking, in fact, might save them   *14*
    from something worse than death.

13

Dear child, if you become wise,
    I'll be one happy parent.
My heart will dance and sing
    to the tuneful truth you'll speak.

14

Don't for a minute envy careless rebels;
    soak yourself in the Fear-of-GOD—
That's where your future lies.
    Then you won't be left with an armload of nothing.

15

Oh listen, dear child—become wise;
    point your life in the right direction.
Don't drink too much wine and get drunk;
    don't eat too much food and get fat.
Drunks and gluttons will end up on skid row,
    in a stupor and dressed in rags.

BUY WISDOM, EDUCATION, INSIGHT

16

Listen with respect to the father who raised you,
    and when your mother grows old, don't neglect her.

Buy truth—don't sell it for love or money;
    buy wisdom, buy education, buy insight.
Parents rejoice when their children turn out well;
    wise children become proud parents.
So make your father happy!
    Make your mother proud!

17

Dear child, I want your full attention;
    please do what I show you.

A whore is a bottomless pit;
    a loose woman can get you in deep trouble fast.
She'll take you for all you've got;
    she's worse than a pack of thieves.

18

Who are the people who are always crying the blues?
    Who do you know who reeks of self-pity?
Who keeps getting beat up for no reason at all?
    Whose eyes are bleary and bloodshot?
It's those who spend the night with a bottle,
    for whom drinking is serious business.
Don't judge wine by its label,
    or its bouquet, or its full-bodied flavor.
Judge it rather by the hangover it leaves you with—
    the splitting headache, the queasy stomach.
Do you really prefer seeing double,
    with your speech all slurred,

Reeling and seasick,
    drunk as a sailor?
"They hit me," you'll say, "but it didn't hurt;
    they beat on me, but I didn't feel a thing.
When I'm sober enough to manage it,
    bring me another drink!"

24

INTELLIGENCE OUTRANKS MUSCLE

19

Don't envy bad people;
    don't even want to be around them.
All they think about is causing a disturbance;
    all they talk about is making trouble.

20

It takes wisdom to build a house,
    and understanding to set it on a firm foundation;
It takes knowledge to furnish its rooms
    with fine furniture and beautiful draperies.

21

It's better to be wise than strong;
    intelligence outranks muscle any day.
Strategic planning is the key to warfare;
    to win, you need a lot of good counsel.

22

Wise conversation is way over the head of fools;
    in a serious discussion they haven't a clue.

23

The person who's always cooking up some evil
soon gets a reputation as prince of rogues.
Fools incubate sin;
cynics desecrate beauty.

RESCUE THE PERISHING

24

If you fall to pieces in a crisis,
there wasn't much to you in the first place.

25

Rescue the perishing;
don't hesitate to step in and help.
If you say, "Hey, that's none of my business,"
will that get you off the hook?
Someone is watching you closely, you know—
Someone not impressed with weak excuses.

26

Eat honey, dear child—it's good for you—
and delicacies that melt in your mouth.
Likewise knowledge,
and wisdom for your soul—
Get that and your future's secured,
your hope is on solid rock.

27

Don't interfere with good people's lives;
don't try to get the best of them.

No matter how many times you trip them up,
>God-loyal people don't stay down long;
Soon they're up on their feet,
>while the wicked end up flat on their faces.

28

Don't laugh when your enemy falls;
>don't crow over his collapse.
GOD might see, and become very provoked,
>and then take pity on his plight.

29

Don't bother your head with braggarts
>or wish you could succeed like the wicked.
Those people have no future at all;
>they're headed down a dead-end street.

30

Fear GOD, dear child—respect your leaders;
>don't be defiant or mutinous.
Without warning your life can turn upside-down,
>and who knows how or when it might happen?

MORE SAYINGS OF THE WISE

AN HONEST ANSWER

It's wrong, very wrong,
>to go along with injustice.

Whoever whitewashes the wicked
    gets a black mark in the history books,
25 But whoever exposes the wicked
    will be thanked and rewarded.

An honest answer
    is like a warm hug.

First plant your fields;
    then build your barn.

Don't talk about your neighbors behind their backs—
    no slander or gossip, please.
29 Don't say to anyone, "I'll get back at you for what you did to me.
    I'll make you pay for what you did!"

One day I walked by the field of an old lazybones,
    and then passed the vineyard of a lout;
They were overgrown with weeds,
    thick with thistles, all the fences broken down.
I took a long look and pondered what I saw;
    the fields preached me a sermon and I listened:
"A nap here, a nap there, a day off here, a day off there,
    sit back, take it easy—do you know what comes next?
Just this: You can look forward to a dirt-poor life,
    with poverty as your permanent houseguest!"

FURTHER WISE SAYINGS OF SOLOMON

25

THE RIGHT WORD AT THE RIGHT TIME

There are also these proverbs of Solomon,
    collected by scribes of Hezekiah, king of Judah.

God delights in concealing things;
    scientists delight in discovering things.

Like the horizons for breadth and the ocean for depth,
    the understanding of a good leader is broad and deep.

Remove impurities from the silver
    and the silversmith can craft a fine chalice;
Remove the wicked from leadership
    and authority will be credible and God-honoring.

Don't work yourself into the spotlight;
    don't push your way into the place of prominence.
It's better to be promoted to a place of honor
    than face humiliation by being demoted.

Don't jump to conclusions—there may be
    a perfectly good explanation for what you just saw.

In the heat of an argument,
    don't betray confidences;

Word is sure to get around,
    and no one will trust you.

The right word at the right time
    is like a custom-made piece of jewelry,

And a wise friend's timely reprimand
    is like a gold ring slipped on your finger.

Reliable friends who do what they say
    are like cool drinks in sweltering heat—refreshing!

Like billowing clouds that bring no rain
    is the person who talks big but never produces.

Patient persistence pierces through indifference;
    gentle speech breaks down rigid defenses.

A Person Without Self-Control

When you're given a box of candy, don't gulp it all down;
    eat too much chocolate and you'll make yourself sick;
And when you find a friend, don't outwear your welcome;
    show up at all hours and he'll soon get fed up.

Anyone who tells lies against the neighbors
    in court or on the street is a loose cannon.

Trusting a double-crosser when you're in trouble
    is like biting down on an abscessed tooth.

Singing light songs to the heavyhearted
    is like pouring salt in their wounds.

If you see your enemy hungry, go buy him lunch;
    if he's thirsty, bring him a drink.
Your generosity will surprise him with goodness,
    and GOD will look after you.

A north wind brings stormy weather,
    and a gossipy tongue stormy looks.

Better to live alone in a tumbledown shack
    than share a mansion with a nagging spouse.

Like a cool drink of water when you're worn out and weary
    is a letter from a long-lost friend.

A good person who gives in to a bad person
    is a muddied spring, a polluted well.

It's not smart to stuff yourself with sweets,
    nor is glory piled on glory good for you.

A person without self-control
    is like a house with its doors and windows knocked out.

26

FOOLS RECYCLE SILLINESS

We no more give honors to fools
    than pray for snow in summer or rain during harvest.

Proverbs 26:2

You have as little to fear from an undeserved curse
    as from the dart of a wren or the swoop of a swallow.

A whip for the racehorse, a tiller for the sailboat—
    and a stick for the back of fools!

4   Don't respond to the stupidity of a fool;
    you'll only look foolish yourself.

5   Answer a fool in simple terms
    so he doesn't get a swelled head.

You're only asking for trouble
    when you send a message by a fool.

A proverb quoted by fools
    is limp as a wet noodle.

Putting a fool in a place of honor
    is like setting a mud brick on a marble column.

To ask a moron to quote a proverb
    is like putting a scalpel in the hands of a drunk.

Hire a fool or a drunk
    and you shoot yourself in the foot.

As a dog eats its own vomit,
    so fools recycle silliness.

See that man who thinks he's so smart?
> You can expect far more from a fool than from him.

Loafers say, "It's dangerous out there!
> Tigers are prowling the streets!"
> and then pull the covers back over their heads.

Just as a door turns on its hinges,
> so a lazybones turns back over in bed.

A shiftless sluggard puts his fork in the pie,
> but is too lazy to lift it to his mouth.

LIKE GLAZE ON CRACKED POTTERY

Dreamers fantasize their self-importance;
> they think they are smarter
> than a whole college faculty.

You grab a mad dog by the ears
> when you butt into a quarrel that's none of your business.

People who shrug off deliberate deceptions,
> saying, "I didn't mean it, I was only joking,"
Are worse than careless campers
> who walk away from smoldering campfires.

When you run out of wood, the fire goes out;
> when the gossip ends, the quarrel dies down.

Proverbs 26:21

A quarrelsome person in a dispute
    is like kerosene thrown on a fire.

Listening to gossip is like eating cheap candy;
    do you want junk like that in your belly?

Smooth talk from an evil heart
    is like glaze on cracked pottery.

Your enemy shakes hands and greets you like an old friend,
    all the while conniving against you.
When he speaks warmly to you, don't believe him for a minute;
    he's just waiting for the chance to rip you off.
No matter how cunningly he conceals his malice,
    eventually his evil will be exposed in public.

Malice backfires;
    spite boomerangs.

Liars hate their victims;
    flatterers sabotage trust.

27

YOU DON'T KNOW TOMORROW

Don't brashly announce what you're going to do tomorrow;
    you don't know the first thing about tomorrow.

Don't call attention to yourself;
    let others do that for you.

Carrying a log across your shoulders
    while you're hefting a boulder with your arms
Is nothing compared to the burden
    of putting up with a fool.

We're blasted by anger and swamped by rage,
    but who can survive jealousy?

A spoken reprimand is better
    than approval that's never expressed.

The wounds from a lover are worth it;
    kisses from an enemy do you in.

When you've stuffed yourself, you refuse dessert;
    when you're starved, you could eat a horse.

People who won't settle down, wandering hither and yon,
    are like restless birds, flitting to and fro.

Just as lotions and fragrance give sensual delight,
    a sweet friendship refreshes the soul.

Don't leave your friends or your parents' friends
    and run home to your family when things get rough;
Better a nearby friend
    than a distant family.

Become wise, dear child, and make me happy;
    then nothing the world throws my way will upset me.

A prudent person sees trouble coming and ducks;
    a simpleton walks in blindly and is clobbered.

Hold tight to collateral on any loan to a stranger;
    be wary of accepting what a transient has pawned.

If you wake your friend in the early morning
    by shouting "Rise and shine!"
It will sound to him
    more like a curse than a blessing.

A nagging spouse is like
    the drip, drip, drip of a leaky faucet;
You can't turn it off,
    and you can't get away from it.

YOUR FACE MIRRORS YOUR HEART

You use steel to sharpen steel,
    and one friend sharpens another.

If you care for your orchard, you'll enjoy its fruit;
    if you honor your boss, you'll be honored.

Just as water mirrors your face,
    so your face mirrors your heart.

Hell has a voracious appetite,
    and lust just never quits.

The purity of silver and gold is tested
    by putting them in the fire;
The purity of human hearts is tested
    by giving them a little fame.

Pound on a fool all you like—
    you can't pound out foolishness.

Know your sheep by name;
    carefully attend to your flocks;
(Don't take them for granted;
    possessions don't last forever, you know.)
And then, when the crops are in
    and the harvest is stored in the barns,
You can knit sweaters from lambs' wool,
    and sell your goats for a profit;
There will be plenty of milk and meat
    to last your family through the winter.

28

IF YOU DESERT GOD'S LAW

The wicked are edgy with guilt, ready to run off
    even when no one's after them;
Honest people are relaxed and confident,
    bold as lions.

When the country is in chaos,
    everybody has a plan to fix it—

Proverbs 28:2

But it takes a leader of real understanding
    to straighten things out.

The wicked who oppress the poor
    are like a hailstorm that beats down the harvest.

If you desert God's law, you're free to embrace depravity;
    if you love God's law, you fight for it tooth and nail.

Justice makes no sense to the evilminded;
    those who seek GOD know it inside and out.

It's better to be poor and direct
    than rich and crooked.

Practice God's law—get a reputation for wisdom;
    hang out with a loose crowd—embarrass your family.

Get as rich as you want
    through cheating and extortion,
But eventually some friend of the poor
    is going to give it all back to them.

God has no use for the prayers
    of the people who won't listen to him.

Lead good people down a wrong path
    and you'll come to a bad end;
        do good and you'll be rewarded for it.

The rich think they know it all,
    but the poor can see right through them.

When good people are promoted, everything is great,
    but when the bad are in charge, watch out!

You can't whitewash your sins and get by with it;
    you find mercy by admitting and leaving them.

A tenderhearted person lives a blessed life;
    a hardhearted person lives a hard life.

Lions roar and bears charge—
    and the wicked lord it over the poor.

Among leaders who lack insight, abuse abounds,
    but for one who hates corruption, the future is bright.

A murderer haunted by guilt
    is doomed—there's no helping him.

Walk straight—live well and be saved;
    a devious life is a doomed life.

DOING GREAT HARM IN SEEMINGLY HARMLESS WAYS

Work your garden—you'll end up with plenty of food;
    play and party—you'll end up with an empty plate.

Committed and persistent work pays off;
    get-rich-quick schemes are ripoffs.

Playing favorites is always a bad thing;
    you can do great harm in seemingly harmless ways.

A miser in a hurry to get rich
    doesn't know that he'll end up broke.

In the end, serious reprimand is appreciated
    far more than bootlicking flattery.

Anyone who robs father and mother
    and says, "So, what's wrong with that?"
    is worse than a pirate.

A grasping person stirs up trouble,
    but trust in GOD brings a sense of well-being.

If you think you know it all, you're a fool for sure;
    real survivors learn wisdom from others.

Be generous to the poor—you'll never go hungry;
    shut your eyes to their needs, and run a gauntlet of curses.

When corruption takes over, good people go underground,
    but when the crooks are thrown out, it's safe to come out.

29

IF PEOPLE CAN'T SEE WHAT GOD IS DOING

For people who hate discipline
    and only get more stubborn,

There'll come a day when life tumbles in and they break,
    but by then it'll be too late to help them.

When good people run things, everyone is glad,
    but when the ruler is bad, everyone groans.

If you love wisdom, you'll delight your parents,
    but you'll destroy their trust if you run with whores.

A leader of good judgment gives stability;
    an exploiting leader leaves a trail of waste.

A flattering neighbor is up to no good;
    he's probably planning to take advantage of you.

Evil people fall into their own traps;
    good people run the other way, glad to escape.

The good-hearted understand what it's like to be poor;
    the hardhearted haven't the faintest idea.

A gang of cynics can upset a whole city;
    a group of sages can calm everyone down.

A sage trying to work things out with a fool
    gets only scorn and sarcasm for his trouble.

Murderers hate honest people;
    moral folks encourage them.

A fool lets it all hang out;
    a sage quietly mulls it over.

When a leader listens to malicious gossip,
    all the workers get infected with evil.

The poor and their abusers have at least something in common:
    they can both *see*—their sight GOD's gift!

Leadership gains authority and respect
    when the voiceless poor are treated fairly.

Wise discipline imparts wisdom;
    spoiled adolescents embarrass their parents.

When degenerates take charge, crime runs wild,
    but the righteous will eventually observe their collapse.

Discipline your children; you'll be glad you did—
    they'll turn out delightful to live with.

If people can't see what God is doing,
    they stumble all over themselves;
But when they attend to what he reveals,
    they are most blessed.

It takes more than talk to keep workers in line;
    mere words go in one ear and out the other.

Observe the people who always talk before they think—
    even simpletons are better off than they are.

If you let people treat you like a doormat,
    you'll be quite forgotten in the end.

Angry people stir up a lot of discord;
    the intemperate stir up trouble.

Pride lands you flat on your face;
    humility prepares you for honors.

Befriend an outlaw
    and become an enemy to yourself.
When the victims cry out,
    you'll be included in their curses
    if you're a coward to their cause in court.

The fear of human opinion disables;
    trusting in GOD protects you from that.

Everyone tries to get help from the leader,
    but only GOD will give us justice.

Good people can't stand the sight of deliberate evil;
    the wicked can't stand the sight of well-chosen goodness.

THE WORDS OF AGUR BEN YAKEH

30

GOD? WHO NEEDS HIM?

The skeptic swore, "There is no God!
    No God!—I can do anything I want!
I'm more animal than human;

so-called human intelligence escapes me.
I flunked 'wisdom.'
  I see no evidence of a holy God.
Has anyone ever seen Anyone
  climb into Heaven and take charge?
  grab the winds and control them?
  gather the rains in his bucket?
  stake out the ends of the earth?
Just tell me his name, tell me the names of his sons.
  Come on now—tell me!"

The believer replied, "Every promise of God proves true;
  he protects everyone who runs to him for help.
So don't second-guess him;
  he might take you to task and show up your lies."

And then he prayed, "God, I'm asking for two things
  before I die; don't refuse me—
Banish lies from my lips
  and liars from my presence.
Give me enough food to live on,
  neither too much nor too little.
If I'm too full, I might get independent,
  saying, 'God? Who needs him?'
If I'm poor, I might steal
  and dishonor the name of my God."

✠

Don't blow the whistle on your fellow workers
    behind their backs;
They'll accuse you of being underhanded,
    and then *you'll* be the guilty one!

Don't curse your father
    or fail to bless your mother.

Don't imagine yourself to be quite presentable
    when you haven't had a bath in weeks.

Don't be stuck-up
    and think you're better than everyone else.

Don't be greedy,
    merciless and cruel as wolves,
Tearing into the poor and feasting on them,
    shredding the needy to pieces only to discard them.

A leech has twin daughters
    named "Gimme" and "Gimme more."

FOUR INSATIABLES

Three things are never satisfied,
    no, there are four that never say, "That's enough,
        thank you!"—

        hell,
        a barren womb,
        a parched land,
        a forest fire.

Proverbs 30:17

✝

An eye that disdains a father
    and despises a mother—
that eye will be plucked out by wild vultures
    and consumed by young eagles.

FOUR MYSTERIES

Three things amaze me,
    no, four things I'll never understand—

        how an eagle flies so high in the sky,
        how a snake glides over a rock,
        how a ship navigates the ocean,
        why adolescents act the way they do.

✝

Here's how a prostitute operates:
    she has sex with her client,
Takes a bath,
    then asks, "Who's next?"

FOUR INTOLERABLES

Three things are too much for even the earth to bear,
    yes, four things shake its foundations—

        when the janitor becomes the boss,
        when a fool gets rich,

when a whore is voted "woman of the year,"
when a "girlfriend" replaces a faithful wife.

FOUR SMALL WONDERS

There are four small creatures,
    wisest of the wise they are—

> ants—frail as they are,
>   get plenty of food in for the winter;
> marmots—vulnerable as they are,
>   manage to arrange for rock-solid homes;
> locusts—leaderless insects,
>   yet they strip the field like an army regiment;
> lizards—easy enough to catch,
>   but they sneak past vigilant palace guards.

FOUR DIGNITARIES

There are three solemn dignitaries,
    four that are impressive in their bearing—

> a lion, king of the beasts, deferring to none;
> a rooster, proud and strutting;
> a billy goat;
> a head of state in stately procession.

☩

If you're dumb enough to call attention to yourself
    by offending people and making rude gestures,

Don't be surprised if someone bloodies your nose.
　　Churned milk turns into butter;
　　riled emotions turn into fist fights.

31

SPEAK OUT FOR JUSTICE

The words of King Lemuel,
　　the strong advice his mother gave him:

"Oh, son of mine, what can you be thinking of!
　　Child whom I bore! The son I dedicated to God!
Don't dissipate your virility on fortune-hunting women,
　　promiscuous women who shipwreck leaders.

"Leaders can't afford to make fools of themselves,
　　gulping wine and swilling beer,
Lest, hung over, they don't know right from wrong,
　　and the people who depend on them are hurt.
Use wine and beer only as sedatives,
　　to kill the pain and dull the ache
Of the terminally ill,
　　for whom life is a living death.

"Speak up for the people who have no voice,
　　for the rights of all the down-and-outers.
Speak out for justice!
　　Stand up for the poor and destitute!"

94

Hymn to a Good Wife

A good woman is hard to find,
    and worth far more than diamonds.
Her husband trusts her without reserve,
    and never has reason to regret it.
Never spiteful, she treats him generously
    all her life long.
She shops around for the best yarns and cottons,
    and enjoys knitting and sewing.
She's like a trading ship that sails to faraway places
    and brings back exotic surprises.
She's up before dawn, preparing breakfast
    for her family and organizing her day.
She looks over a field and buys it,
    then, with money she's put aside, plants a garden.
First thing in the morning, she dresses for work,
    rolls up her sleeves, eager to get started.
She senses the worth of her work,
    is in no hurry to call it quits for the day.
She's skilled in the crafts of home and hearth,
    diligent in homemaking.
She's quick to assist anyone in need,
    reaches out to help the poor.
She doesn't worry about her family when it snows;
    their winter clothes are all mended and ready to wear.
She makes her own clothing,
    and dresses in colorful linens and silks.
Her husband is greatly respected
    when he deliberates with the city fathers.

Proverbs 31:24

She designs gowns and sells them,
> brings the sweaters she knits to the dress shops.

Her clothes are well-made and elegant,
> and she always faces tomorrow with a smile.

When she speaks she has something worthwhile to say,
> and she always says it kindly.

She keeps an eye on everyone in her household,
> and keeps them all busy and productive.

Her children respect and bless her;
> her husband joins in with words of praise:

"Many women have done wonderful things,
> but you've outclassed them all!"

Charm can mislead and beauty soon fades.
> The woman to be admired and praised
> is the woman who lives in the Fear-of-GOD.

Give her everything she deserves!
> Festoon her life with praises!